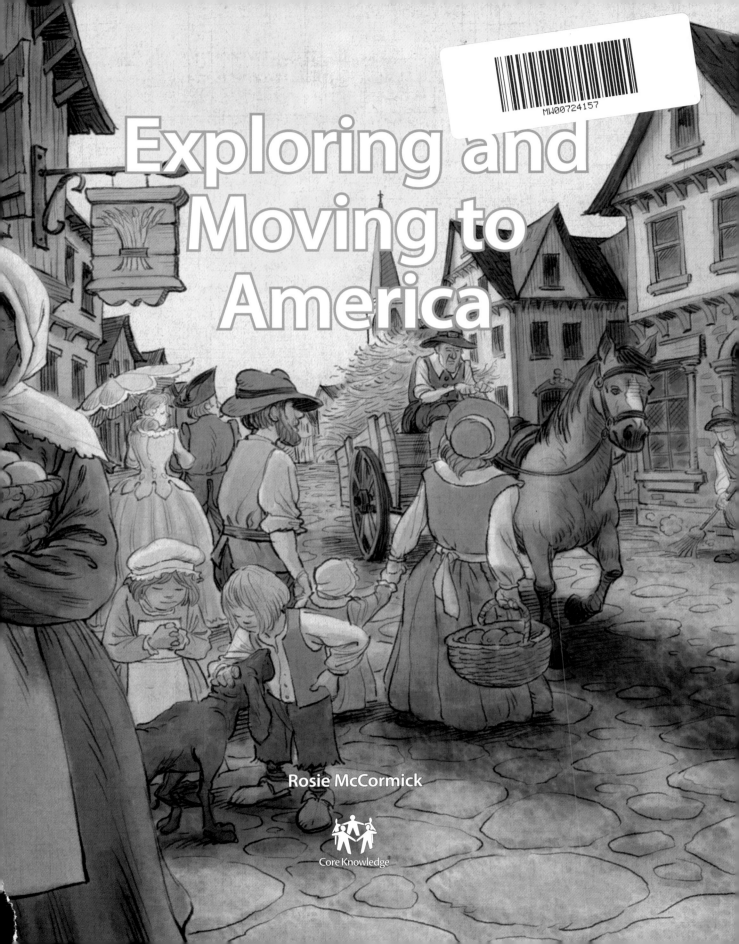

Exploring and Moving to America

Rosie McCormick

Core Knowledge

ISBN: 978-1-68380-370-6

Exploring and Moving to America

Table of Contents

Christopher Columbus: A Young Adventurer

When Christopher Columbus was a boy, he and his younger brother loved to spend time at the dock in the Italian city of Genoa, where they lived. They watched the ships sail in and out.

They watched as the sailors unloaded boxes filled with silk cloth and spices. They dreamed of being sailors too!

When Christopher was fourteen years old, he got a job on a ship, carrying messages from the captain to the sailors. One year later, he was hired as a ship's helper—and then as a sailor. His dream of adventure at sea was coming true.

His brother learned to make maps, and together they hoped to sail far away.

Long ago, people didn't know about all the continents and oceans. Some people thought that Earth was flat and that if a ship sailed too far across the ocean, it would fall off the edge. But others, including Christopher, believed that Earth was round like a ball.

Christopher Has an Idea

Why did people, such as Christopher Columbus and his brother, want to set off on long voyages? The main reason was that people wanted to trade, or buy and sell, such things as spices and silk that were not found in Europe. Trade could make people rich!

In Christopher Columbus's time, there were no refrigerators to keep food fresh. Europeans often ate food, especially meat, that was not fresh. People used spices, such as cloves, pepper, cinnamon, and nutmeg, to make food taste better.

Many of these spices could only be found in a faraway part of the world that Europeans called "the Indies." Today, this part of the world is known as Asia.

A voyage to the Indies and back again was long and dangerous. After sailing part of the way across seas or oceans, some people then carried goods on camels across hot, sandy deserts. Many times they were robbed, or got lost, or ran out of water.

Sailing ship

Christopher had an idea. If Earth was round, maybe he could sail west around the world and reach the Indies that way. The whole voyage could be made by ship across the Atlantic Ocean, with no need to travel across hot, dry deserts.

Many more spices and other goods could be carried on ships than on camels. Camels were called "ships of the desert."

Today, we know that if you sail west across the Atlantic Ocean from Europe, you reach the Americas, or North and South America. But of course Christopher didn't know this. Long ago, many people thought there was nothing but ocean if you sailed west.

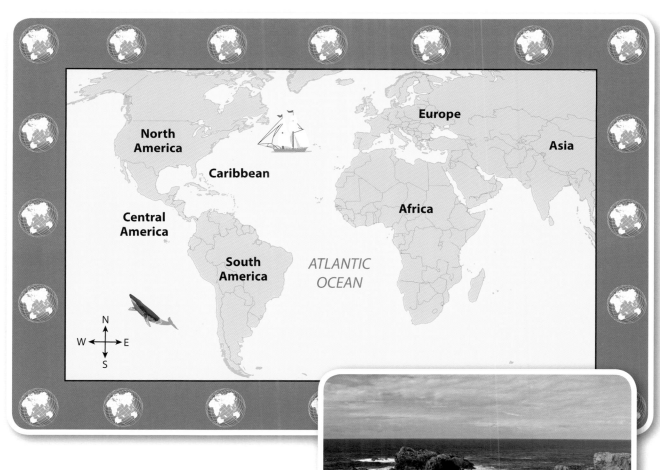

Christopher needed someone to believe he could sail across the Atlantic Ocean—the second largest ocean on Earth.

CHAPTER 3

Christopher Sails West

For many, many years, Christopher planned his voyage. He also searched for someone rich enough to pay for this risky adventure. Finally, he had the chance to meet King Ferdinand and Queen Isabella of Spain.

He told them about his idea of reaching the Indies by sailing west across the Atlantic Ocean.

The Spanish king and queen did want to find an easier way for their ships to get to the Indies. They wanted to trade their cloth, glass, and tools for spices, silk, jewels, and gold. Spain would become rich if Christopher's plan worked.

King Ferdinand and Queen Isabella decided to pay for the voyage. Now Christopher could start his great adventure!

The king and queen of Spain gave Christopher three ships: the *Niña*, the *Pinta*, and the *Santa Maria*. Each ship had a captain. Christopher Columbus was the captain of the *Santa Maria*.

The three ships were small, but they were strong enough to sail across the stormy waters of the Atlantic Ocean.

Columbus found sailors who wanted to go with him to the Indies. They loaded the ships with enough food and water to last a year, as well as with things they could trade. They also took firewood, cooking pots, medicines, fishing lines, swords, and guns. When everything was ready, they set off across the wide, blue ocean.

The Voyage West

The three ships sailed across the ocean. The sailors were not sure of what they might find. There might be pirates or even sea monsters. If things went wrong, no one would be able to help them.

Still, the sailors kept busy. They cleaned the decks, and they fished in the ocean.

Each day, two or three sailors cooked a meal for everyone on their ship. At night, the sailors slept on the deck. There were no beds. Only the three captains had their own small cabins. On stormy nights, the men tied themselves to the ship's rails so they wouldn't fall into the ocean.

Christopher and his men sailed for many weeks, but they did not find any land. The men began to be afraid. What if Earth really was flat, and they sailed right off the edge? What if they ran out of food and water in the middle of the ocean?

The sailors wanted to return home, but Christopher was still sure his plan would work.

Then one day, small birds flew alongside the ship. The sailors knew that small birds often flew near land. Soon after, a sailor spotted something. "Land! Land!" he shouted. After almost two months, the sailors were excited to see a sandy beach and beautiful green trees. They had found an island. In his diary, Christopher wrote down the date: October 12, 1492.

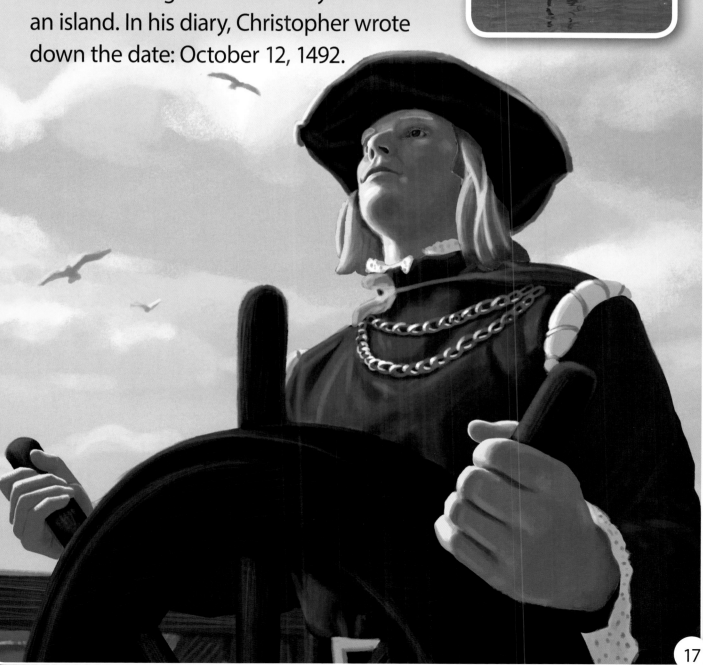

Seabird

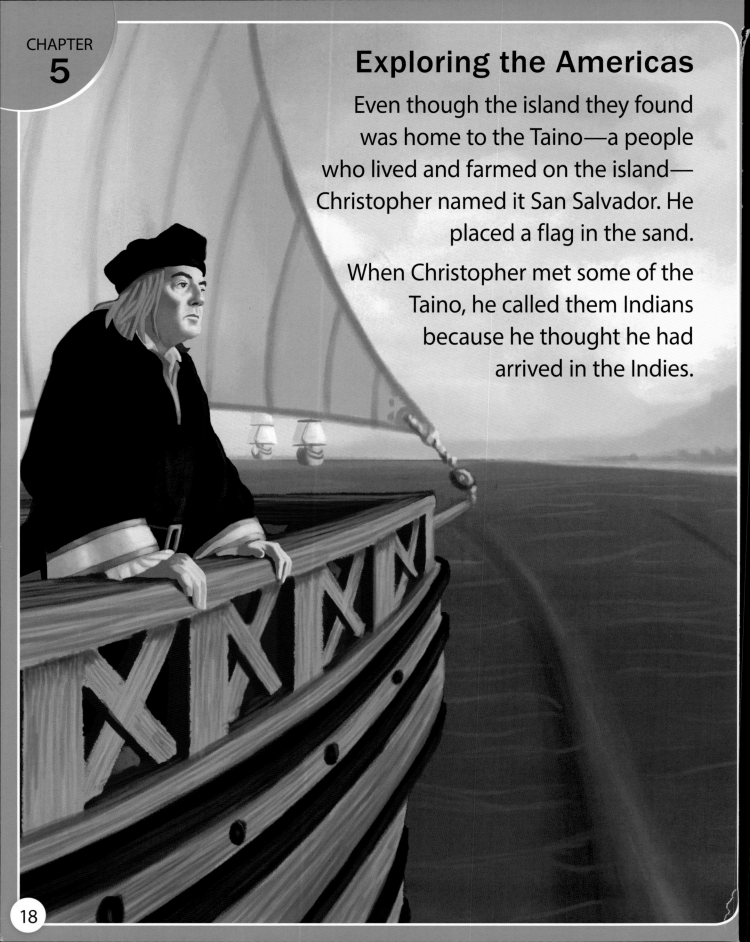

Exploring the Americas

Even though the island they found was home to the Taino—a people who lived and farmed on the island—Christopher named it San Salvador. He placed a flag in the sand.

When Christopher met some of the Taino, he called them Indians because he thought he had arrived in the Indies.

Christopher and his men spent a few months exploring other islands, including Cuba. The Taino lived on these islands too.

The islands had palm trees and white sand. Christopher and his men collected some gold, tobacco plants, pineapples, and wild turkeys to take back to Spain.

When Christopher arrived back in Spain, he was treated as a hero. The king and queen were happy with him. They agreed to pay for more ships so that he could sail back across the ocean. Christopher made four more voyages across the ocean looking for gold, spices, and jewels.

The Pilgrims Search for a New Home

More than one hundred years after Christopher Columbus sailed across the Atlantic Ocean, another group of Europeans also set off. They were traveling to what is today the United States of America.

Their story is a little different from that of Christopher Columbus. Let's meet them and find out about the adventures they had.

Elizabeth stood with her parents ready to board a ship named the *Mayflower*. Elizabeth and her family were leaving Plymouth, England, to sail to America. Elizabeth, her parents, and friends were known as Pilgrims.

The Pilgrims were making this voyage so that they could live in a place where they could worship God in their own way.

The *Mayflower* had been loaded with things the Pilgrims would need for the voyage, and for when they arrived. There were axes and saws for building homes, hooks and lines for fishing, seeds for their gardens, and warm clothes for the winter. There were also barrels of water, dried meat, vegetables, biscuits, and cheese.

As the *Mayflower* sailed away, leaving England behind, Elizabeth began to explore the ship. The first thing she noticed was that it was crowded. Below deck was dark and stuffy.

In the darkness she saw that there were hammocks for people to sleep in. Even though the voyage would be long and dangerous, Elizabeth was excited!

On Board the *Mayflower*

Elizabeth spent much of her time exploring the ship. She watched as sailors pulled on ropes to raise large, cloth sails. When the sails puffed out in the wind, the ship moved faster over the waves.

Soon the weather changed, and strong winds began to blow. Giant waves crashed against the ship, and rain leaked below deck, soaking the travelers' clothes and beds. The *Mayflower* tossed from side to side. The Pilgrims were afraid that the ship would sink. Elizabeth was no longer excited to be sailing to their new home.

Long weeks went by. The Pilgrims got tired of living in such a small space. People were getting sick. Then, early one morning, a sailor up in the crow's nest yelled, "Land! I see land!" All of the Pilgrims rushed up on deck to see. Their voyage was almost over!

CHAPTER 8

The Pilgrims Work Hard to Survive

Some of the Pilgrims set off first to find a good place to settle. They finally chose a place they called Plymouth, after the town they had left behind.

Elizabeth couldn't help but wonder if there would be strange creatures in the forests. Would the Wampanoag and other Native Americans welcome them?

The Pilgrims had arrived just as the weather was turning cold. They needed to build homes as quickly as they could. They worked hard cutting down trees. They would use the wood to build their homes. Not only was it getting cold, they were worried they might run out of food. To stay warm, the women and children stayed on board the *Mayflower*.

During that first winter, many of the Pilgrims became sick and died. It was a sad time for the Pilgrims. By springtime, many of the Pilgrims were able to move into their new homes. It would soon be time to plant crops so that they would have food to eat.

Then one day, a man came to visit the Pilgrims. His name was Squanto, and he was a Native American. Squanto could speak English. Even though the Pilgrims had settled on Native American land, Squanto helped them plant crops, such as beans, corn, pumpkins, and other vegetables.

Thanks to Squanto, the crops grew well. Soon it was time to harvest them, and to celebrate.

The Pilgrims decided to have a feast of thanksgiving. They invited their Native American friends. At the feast, people ate deer, turkey, corn, beans, pumpkins, and freshly baked bread. They gave thanks for the food they had to eat. Then everyone enjoyed an afternoon of fun and games.

American Independence

For many years, the Pilgrims and other settlers lived happily in their new home. Because many of these new settlers were from England, they were happy to follow some English laws, as well as to make their own rules. But eventually things began to go wrong.

When King George III and his parliament in England passed new laws that seemed very unfair, the settlers became angry. Some people protested. American leaders decided to hold a meeting to decide what to do next.

The American leaders wrote a long letter to King George III explaining why they felt he and his parliament were being unfair. The letter was called the Declaration of Independence. The letter explained that the Americans wanted to make many of their own laws. They did not want to follow all of the laws made by the king.

King George III did not agree with the Declaration of Independence, and he sent his army to fight the Americans. The Americans had a great leader named George Washington. He helped America defeat King George's army.

George Washington

Today we celebrate America's birthday on July 4, the day the Declaration of Independence was signed.

Taken to America

There is another story about moving to America. This is the story of people from different parts of Africa who were forced onto ships and taken to America. In America, they became enslaved. This is a very sad story, but it is one we must never forget.

People from Africa were taken to America to work on large farms. Because they were enslaved, they were not free. They did not have rights. Enslaved workers were not paid for the hard work they did. Americans today are not proud of this time of slavery.

Most of the farms that used enslaved workers were in the southern part of America. Back then there were no machines to do the hard work. Enslaved workers did it instead.

They worked in the fields planting and picking crops. They carried water, fixed fences, and took care of farm animals.

Enslaved children couldn't go to school to learn how to read and write. Families were often broken up as farm owners sold children or parents.

Many people in America knew that slavery was wrong. They knew that America could not be truly free until everyone was free. But it took time and another war for the enslaved to win their freedom.

Today it is important to remember the many African Americans who never got the chance to be free.

CKHG™

Core Knowledge HISTORY AND GEOGRAPHY™

Editorial Directors

Linda Bevilacqua and Rosie McCormick

Subject Matter Expert

J. Chris Arndt, PhD, Department of History, James Madison University

Illustration and Photo Credits